A Life Story
Ministry in an Age of Change

Henry E. Roberts

EnerPower Press
Cantonment, Florida
2024

Copyright © 2024, Henry E. Roberts. All rights reserved.

Unless otherwise indicated, scripture quotations are from the Revised Standard Version of the Bible, copyright 1952 [2nd edition, 1971] by the Division of Christian Education of the National Council of the Churches of Christ in the United States of America. Used by permission. All rights reserved.

Cover Design: Jeb Hunt

ISBN: 978-1-63199-916-1
eISBN: 978-1-63199-917-8
Library of Congress Control Number: 2024920149

EnerPower Press
an Imprint of Energion Publications
1241 Conference Rd
Cantonment, FL 32533

(850) 525-3916
pubs@energion.com

To my family,
To those living,
To those who have died,
And those yet to be born,
I just wanted to tell you what it was like.
I wanted you to know what I felt,
What I did,
And what I tried to be.

I wanted you to know
How my story was not hard,
But how it was meaningful.
I hope you will tell others your story.
Tell them you existed.
Tell them about how you lived,
And above all,
Tell them all how much you were loved.

Table of Contents

Introduction
1

Chapter 1
The Black Belt
1943-1960
7

Chapter 2
Answering God's Call
1960-1970
23

Chapter 3
Preaching, Praying, and Pastoral Care
1970-1980
59

Chapter 4
The Florida Years
1980-2006
77

Conclusion
Eighty and Beyond
111

Epilogue
115

Introduction

In our retirement years, my wife, Jane, and I have begun to write some of our life stories. She is writing about her family, a project she has called "Mammy Stories" that emerged out of her experiences with her beloved grandmother. Her sweetly meandering narratives based on clear childhood memories are wonderful and through these stories, others will remember her family long after we have passed.

After forty-three years in the appointive ministry of the United Methodist Church and seven years as a fundraiser in the Catholic healthcare field, I retired from full-time ministry and started examining why and how I have spent the past five decades. I began to write in my personal journal and reflect on what I wanted our children and grandchildren and family and friends to know about the life Jane and I have lived together, of our major life events, of the fascinating people we met, of the trips we took, of the unique ministry opportunities God gave us during the half-century of our marriage. We have always looked upon our marriage as part of our vocation. A career has to do with jobs that provide financial and psychological benefits, but a vocation is more of a calling. If your job or career isn't working for you, you choose a different one. One's vocation is what determines what you do with your life.

So much of our adult life has been focused on our education and service in the ministry of Christ, and it seemed that the first claim on my life was always the needs of others—sometimes at the expense of our immediate family. Jane understood my calling from God and accepted the demands of time, energy, and focus, but time commitments were not easy for either of us. During these years she was developing her own unique ministry and career in the counseling field. There were always weddings, funerals, pastoral visits, study, and preparation time for sermons as Sundays seemed to come every other day. I realized that I wanted our children, who would live long after we were gone, to know that Jane and I had served the causes of Christ during a unique time in American history. I wanted them to know that we had given our best to God's kingdom far beyond our immediate needs or desires. Perhaps most importantly, we have sought throughout the years to give to our family members what our parents gave to us—a confident faith in God and an uncompromising desire to follow the way of Christ through a disciplined, servant lifestyle.

The fact is I am very grateful that I have been given by a gracious creator a good life filled with wonderful memories, good health, supportive parents, and opportunities to choose my way in a world that affords a select few with unlimited possibilities. Having now the opportunity to reflect on the careers that we have been involved in over these years is a unique opportunity and gradually I have begun to record some of those memories. As I have spent my adult years doing acts of ministry, preparing for sermons, and counseling individuals who are struggling with life's issues, I find myself exhausted and ready for the retirement years that have now begun. I would not share these stories with anyone for some time because I didn't want to feel any pressure to produce something from my personal musings. I had done enough of that kind of thing over the years in my sermons and other writings. Nevertheless, I have chosen to record some of my thoughts and a perspective that covers the years of my life between 1943 and 2023. I was privileged to serve as a United Methodist minister for a half-century in the Southeast region of the United States. I served during a unique period in American history, a time of immense social change.

    I don't know that the world that we are passing on to our children is any better than the world we received from our parents, but Jane and I want our children to know that because of our commitment to Christ and to each other, we have tried to make a difference in our time in hopes that they will make a difference in theirs. Part of the legacy that I leave is a profound gratitude to God for my calling to be a minister. Our work in God's kingdom has been a shared life experience of love with a lifelong mate and family and service to others in an ever-changing world.

Chapter 1 | The Black Belt

1943-1960

I look back on my formative years with gratitude. I grew up in the small town of Linden, Alabama. It was originally known as *Hohenlinden,* which came from early French farming immigrants remembering Napoleon's victory in Bavaria in 1800, but everyday usage shortened the name. Linden was the county seat of Marengo County, which was in the Black Belt of West Alabama. That regional moniker stemmed from its fertile, black soil, not the skin color of its residents. Even so, most of the people who lived there were Black, but the white minority, of which I was a part, held the power and governing authority.

Pervasive racism firmly segregated the Black and white residents of our small community of less than 2,500 people, but there was nothing equal or fair about such a dysfunctional system. In our separate communities, God did provide many loving parents, teachers, and pastors who helped shape many lives.

I was born on April 14, 1943, in Selma's old Vaughn Memorial Hospital in a whites-only section. I would live in a segregated society—where I was largely oblivious to those who were not like me and my immediate family—for the next twenty years. The few Black babies born that same day at the hospital were carried home within hours, unable to stay overnight with their mothers, because no room had been made available for Black families. Some of those babies might have grown up to participate in the Selma March—the pivotal protest that precipitated the Voting Rights Act of 1965—twenty-two years later.

The first two decades of my journey never carried me far beyond my hometown or the racism inherent in the Old South. As a literal fact, I lived on the edge of "The Ditch," which separated whites from Blacks in Linden. I played cops and robbers with wooden guns and old red-knotted rubber inner tubes as bullets while the Black children from the other side of the ditch walked on bare, cracked feet to the cotton mill or the saw mill or private homes where they would work for chump change to help their families keep from starving.

During those early years, I began to develop an inner confidence that all things were possible. This notion was affirmed in my home by loving parents, by teachers in the schools where I received my education, and by the teachers I saw on Sunday while worshiping at our small Methodist Church. It was like every person in my life and every institution was pulling for me to grow up and serve God and enjoy life. Through relationships with healthy people, the opportunity to play sports of all kinds, and myriad other choices, life helped me stand tall and always seemed to be saying, "Yes, you can!" This was the privilege of living in a whites-first society.

There was a baby girl who was born in her family home about three miles behind our house. Her name was Iona Odessa Johnson, and her story would be vastly different from my life of privilege and opportunity. She took her first breath in a run-down, two-room, brown clapboard shack at the end of a dirt road, the fourth of what would eventually be seventeen children. The only way I knew Iona was because her family worked for mine. Her mother, Chinese Doss Johnson, cleaned our house, while Iona's father scraped a living out of the forests and farms in the area. He and his son Will would bring their mule to our house to cut in a spring garden. A garden was a hobby for us. It was survival for Iona's family.

When Iona was old enough to work, she would accompany her mother to our house to clean. When her mother was having babies or just sick from exhaustion, Iona would come alone. One of her brothers would walk with her from their home along the dirt road to our house to ensure her safety. I seemed to have pretty much everything. Iona seemed to have little to nothing.

We would live three miles from each other at various times in our lives—when we were young and growing up in Linden, when we both went to college in Montgomery, Alabama, and again in Mobile where our children attended separate schools. What I would come to know and appreciate about Iona was that although she lacked the abundant opportunity I had, she possessed a deep and abiding faith that all things came from God. I learned this about Iona when we reconnected a few years ago in Mobile where she had made her home. I looked her up and visited her at her house, and on another visit, we went to dinner and shared a meal and good conversation.

Iona told me she believed that all things—the good and the bad, the laughing days and the hard days—came from God. There were not many laughing days for Iona. The bad days came often, and she lived in fear. Iona held baby number fourteen of her family's seventeen children in her own hands when she was but a child herself. As the infant slipped from her mother's womb, she heard only, "Don't drop the baby!" As a young girl, Iona heard many other things too—insults, harsh judgments, ignorant opinions, and hateful racial slurs. She often wondered what would become of her life and if she was destined to follow in her parents' footsteps. Through it all, however, she believed that God was teaching her to trust in him. Iona was confident that all things would work together for good for those who loved God. And love God she did. Even as she fell asleep hungry, with her sister's feet in her face, she prayed prayers of thanksgiving. With the coming of dawn's light, which was the only light in her family's shack, came Iona's prayers of gratitude for another day.

Famed Congregational minister Henry Ward Beecher once wrote:

> "If one should give me a dish of sand and tell me there were particles of iron in it, I might look for them with my eyes, and search for them with my clumsy fingers, and be unable to detect them, but let me take a magnet, sweep through it, and see how it would draw to itself the almost invisible particles by the mere power of attraction. The thankless heart, like my finger in the sand, discovers no mercies,

but let the thankful heart sweep through the day, and as the magnet finds the iron, so it will find, in every hour, some heavenly blessings; only the iron in God's sand is gold."

Iona had discovered that faith in God was the magnet that finds the metal in the sands of time.

Thanks to a generous, unexpected gift from an aunt who lived in Houston, Texas, Iona would attend her first year of college at Alabama State University in Montgomery. Working with great persistence, she would make it through school in the next four years. With a new education degree, she would not return to the end of the dirt road on the outskirts of Linden but instead moved to Mobile where she made her contribution as a teacher in the Mobile County School System. She also met and married a mathematics instructor at Bishop State Community College and had two beautiful, smart daughters. Iona didn't forget her past. She had only to look down at her hands, scarred from cotton picking as a child, to remember those years. She fought to overcome prejudice and racial hatred, and through education, she rose above her limitations and has given a wonderful life to her children.

Every person has a story that is unique because it has been altered by specific circumstances, rare opportunities, hardships, personal choices and the guidance of the eternal God's purpose and plan. Depending on which side of The Ditch you happen to be born on, your start in life might be more difficult, but that start does not dictate how your story ends. I have learned that it is not only what happens around you that shapes your life but also what goes on inside you and how you respond.

I know I was making decisions in the early years of my development, but until I left home for college, my life was shaped by two very human but wonderful people—a strong father and a forceful and wise mother. Both dealt with life from a Christian perspective and seemed to have unlimited resources.

My dad, James Henry Roberts, was born on January 17, 1911, in a bedroom of a home located beside the Methodist Church in Clanton, Alabama.

The eleventh child in a family of twelve, he would experience the death of a sister in a house fire, the death of his father when he was nine, and the death of his mother one year later. Although the family had at one time been well off and owned two sections of virgin timber in Chilton County, Alabama, as well as a general mercantile store, with the passing of the parents and the Depression, most of its financial and emotional stability was lost. In the early years, my father had lived from "pillar to post", as one would say in the South, meaning that various uncles and aunts would keep him for a limited time and then he would have to move on to the next relative. He never talked much about the hardships, but one day he told me that when he was on the train alone pulling into the Clanton train station from a two-year stay in the North, where he had lived with a distant relative, he told himself, "I am never going back up there again."

My mother, Gladys Mae Williams, was born on December 28, 1910, the second child in a family of six. Her father, Thomas Leonard Williams, worked as the local manager of the Chilton County office of the Alabama Power Company. As a hard worker and a respected member of the community, my grandfather was able to provide stability for my mother and her siblings.

On my mother's side of our family tree, her grandparents, Joseph Lebanon and Leila Ann Williams, lived with their twelve children on a farm in the heart of Chilton County, Alabama. Nine of the children were boys, and three of those boys would become ministers in the Baptist Church. One was a missionary to China, and another was a writer for the Baptist Sunday School Association out of Nashville. One was Dr. Horace Williams, who served as the pastor of the Calvary Baptist Church on the campus of the University of Alabama in Tuscaloosa. It was Uncle Horace who one day in the later days of his life was visiting with our family and handed me ten dimes. He told me that they were all mine except for the first dime, which was God's and I had to put it in the church offering the next Sunday. That was my first introduction to tithing as a life management principle, and it would guide me the rest of my life. Uncle Horace served as Senior Minister of the University Church in Tuscaloosa for twenty-seven years, which means that he taught me not only the value of tithing but also the value of a long-term pastorate.

It was my grandfather, Thomas Williams, who gave my father his first job—working as a lineman—when his money for college ran out and he was forced to leave Auburn University after two years. Upon my dad's return to Chilton County, love blossomed and in time my parents were married. In 1939 they moved to Linden with my brother, Jimmy, their second child. Their first child, Elizabeth Ann, had been stillborn on March 18, 1938, in their home in Clanton. Because of their desire to provide security and stability for their children, they would travel fifty miles to the nearest hospital for my brother's birth and then five years later for me.

By the time I was born, my dad was the local manager of the Alabama Power Company, which meant that he rode across the county in a red company truck, keeping the electricity on, rain or shine, twenty-four seven. My mother was a stay-at-home mom who cared for Dad, my older brother, Jimmy, and me in much the same way. I would often ride with Dad in his truck and watch as he climbed the tall power poles and visited with rural Alabamians, most of whom were dirt poor and on whom, in the 1950s, the Great Depression still seemed to have a death grip.

My family was fortunate. Because my parents had lived through the Great Depression, our lifestyle was frugal but never lacking. We did not suffer. We always had enough of anything and everything that was necessary. We boys never questioned that we were loved; it was like an entitlement. We knew the meaning of hard work and disciplined desires but not deprivation like Iona's family and many others who lived just across The Ditch and down the dirt road from us.

During my formative years, my family laid a spiritual foundation that would support my decision to follow the way of Jesus Christ. My parents faithfully "carried" me to the small Methodist

Church we attended and where my mother, who never had any formal musical training but taught herself to play the piano, was the organist and pianist. They raised me in a home where we prayed at a family table before eating and sharing daily events. I was very involved in our small Methodist Church growing up because that was the way things were in our family. Sunday was church day! We were in church on Sunday morning and Sunday evening, every week, come rain or shine!

When I was 16 years old, I was the President of what was called the Ada Gray Subdistrict. It was composed of the youth fellowship groups of all of the Methodist churches in our area. Each year we would sponsor a "Youth Weekend Revival" and in the spring of 1958, Dr. Andy Gallman, a preacher from the Mississippi Conference, was the chosen preacher for the two day meeting over the weekend. On the final night, Dr. Gallman gave an invitation to come forward, kneel at the altar, and give your heart to Christ. I can still remember that "my heart was strangely warmed" as John Wesley said about his calling and that I was aware that I was moving toward the altar not knowing what was going on. Brother Sam Hudgins, our pastor, knelt down beside me, prayed a prayer, and I cried tears of joy. He said something about "full-time Christian service" and all I knew was that something had happened inside of me that was more powerful than anything I had ever experienced before. That night I did give my life to Christ and devoted myself to whatever he wanted me to do with my life.

When I was in the eleventh grade, almost at the end of my high school years, I announced my decision to choose full-time Christian service. Although religion opened my heart to God, it would take the educational experience of college and changing times to open my eyes to the people of different nationalities, colors, and needs.

I owe my parents a great deal, and they taught me well, particularly my mother. She really managed our family life in the early years. As I remember, she had figured out that I seemed to thrive on praise and ego strokes, and she gave me all I needed of both to get me going. When I was very young, she would brag on me and say things like: "You can polish silver better than anybody in this family. You clean up and organize old storage closets better than anyone I know." I began to develop self-confidence and assurance. I thought to myself, "I am good at organization and cleaning up old messes!" Consequently, I have cleaned up and organized numerous old churches, inefficient organizations, and messy situations all my life. And all because my mother bragged on me as I did the things she needed done.

A few years into our marriage, I was helping Jane clean up the kitchen after one of the many church parties she had hosted, and she said to me, "You know, you can bring order out of chaos in a kitchen so much better than I can or anyone I have ever known." My first reaction was, "You know, she's right. I can clean up a mess better than anyone I know." And then I thought about what she had said and what I was saying to myself and said, "Oh no you don't! I know what you are trying to do, and I'm not going to fall for that old trick. Not this time!"

What I really learned from my mom was that bragging on someone's strengths and praising what they do well is a more effective motivation than criticizing them for their failures. It sure has worked better for me in the recruitment of church volunteer leaders than any other method I learned over the years. Things also seemed to work a little better at home when I remember this early lesson on motivation.

Chapter 2 | Answering God's Call

1960-1970

The 1960s brought many changes to our lives. During this decade I would move away from my hometown of Linden to attend college in Montgomery, fall in love with Elizabeth Jane Strange, and start a family. Most importantly, I would answer God's call to full-time preaching and pastoral service.

I was guided early on by Rev. Sam Huggins when he served as our pastor at Linden Methodist Church. Brother Sam was a humble servant with little education and spoke with a constant left-to-right twitch in his neck and jaw that was very distracting. Even with his limitations, he demonstrated that a minister primarily was called to love his people. Having him as our pastor taught me early on that people did not care how much their preacher knew until they knew how much he cared. Brother Sam was much loved in our little community, and it was through his halting voice that God had called me into the ministry.

Another clergy member in our community who greatly influenced me was a Baptist minister by the name of Joe Patterson. When I was in the eleventh grade, I had tentatively made the decision to enter the ministry, and Rev. Patterson had the dubious honor of being paired with me for my high school's Career Day. A day out of school was my kind of thing, so I was ready when the eventful day began—and little did I know that it would shape my professional life for the next forty-four years.

Rev. Patterson, who was also a Rotarian, welcomed me into his office around 8:30 a.m. one October morning with the question, "Well, what do you want to do?" At seventeen years old, I had no clue and responded like most teenagers: "Whatever." He then said to me that a minister must respond on behalf of God to any human need that occurs in the geographical area where he is called to serve. I had no idea what that meant, but he asked, "Do you know anyone in our community that is in trouble or needs help just now?" I stuttered and stammered and said I had heard that a man who lived on the outskirts of town had killed himself the day before and that I assumed his family might be in great need. Rev. Patterson said he had also heard about that tragedy and although he did not know the family personally, he would find out where they lived, and we would make a visit. I thought, "What? We don't know these folks, and we are going to just show up and knock on their door?" That was exactly what we did.

I was nervous and uneasy, but after a couple of phone calls, we drove unannounced to their home and knocked on the door. When a teary-eyed, overwhelmed-looking woman answered the door, Rev. Patterson introduced us, said we had heard about her husband, and offered to visit and pray with her. The woman broke down in a puddle of tears and confessed that she just did not know what to do, had no minister, and needed any help he could offer. There on the spot they made plans for a funeral, and he scheduled a time to visit with her the next day. Later I learned that Rev. Patterson had some of the women in his church take food to the family and that he led the funeral service at the gravesite.

I share this story because I was amazed by the courage and confident spirit Rev. Patterson demonstrated in knocking on the door of a stranger and offering such a God-like, caring spirit. His example would guide me as I ministered to strangers for the next half-century, offering God's caring love in times of great tragedy. I learned more about pastoral care in that strange visit than I ever learned while earning my master's and doctorate degrees at Emory University's Candler School of Theology.

A footnote to this teaching moment occurred in 2007 when my path crossed with Rev. Patterson's in Panama City, Florida. My friend Charlie Hilton, a successful lawyer and community leader, asked me to go with him to visit his friend who was dying of cancer in a local hospital. When I walked into the room, Rev. Patterson and I were stunned to see each other for the first time in almost 50 years. I learned that he had been asked to leave Linden Baptist Church in the 1960s because he supported caring for the Black residents in our town and welcoming them to his church. During those troubling years, white preachers like Rev. Patterson were treated harshly, called hateful, racist names, and quickly moved from one church to another until they were finally sent "Up North." Sadly, Rev. Patterson's moral courage cost him his career, and he moved to Alaska where he later lost his wife and children in a house fire. Broken in spirit, he left the ministry and had been living in Panama City, operating a small motel, when we reconnected. During that unexpected visit, I thanked Rev. Patterson for what he had taught me so long ago because it had guided my ministry my entire career. I was privileged to lead his funeral. Known only as Joe to a small number of people, Rev. Patterson died with small rewards for his faith and witness, but I was pleased to be with him again in his time of great need. It is strange how God guides our lives and places us in unique situations to represent his caring spirit if we are bold and compassionate enough to knock on the doors of strangers. I am aware that he was one of many ministers in those changing times who lost recognition by the world because of their witness for social justice.

During those developing years, teachers also shaped my life. There was Mrs. Elizabeth Mashburn, who taught me a love of history that would influence my undergraduate and graduate school studies. Mrs. Emily Burge, our student government sponsor, guided me as a young leader as I learned to preside over meetings as president of my high school's student government association. Mrs. Marie Law suggested—pretty strongly, I might add—that I attend a Methodist college in Montgomery, Alabama called Huntingdon, which was a small college with an enrollment of 1200 students. It was an excellent choice for me coming from a rural Alabama background and anticipating going on toward a seminary degree after the college years to prepare for ministry. Jane and I both received an excellent liberal arts education which introduced us to the best of human thought in the fields of literature, philosophy, history, science, and the arts.

Another influential teacher was Walter "Pistol" Henders, our high school coach who taught me to play quarterback for Linden High School's Red Devil football team, first base for the baseball team, and a forward position for the basketball team. He also taught me to "suck it up" and "get the job done." He was tough on all the students who played under his tutorship. Imagine my surprise when I came across an old family box of yellowed memories and found inside a Valentine's Day card addressed to me and signed with the words, "Love you, Coach Henders." I was privileged to be asked by his family to speak at his funeral held in his home church in Crestview, Florida.

At Huntingdon I became president of the freshman class. I have always desired to be a leader in whatever group I was in—either because I thought I could facilitate a meeting in an effective manner or because I liked to lead, not follow. This was a personality trait nourished early in my life that grew stronger as the years passed. To this day, I still find it difficult to sit still in a group or in church or anywhere when someone else is speaking.

It takes nerve and confidence to stand before people time and time again and speak on behalf of God and to assume that you can tell them what is important about their life, what they need to do, and where they need to go. But life has occasionally reminded me that I was not God and only spoke for God. Time and time again, I was brought back to the reality of my importance, which wasn't as big a deal as I sometimes thought it was. Such a character trait was not easy to live with, but Jane has made the best of it—and the best of me—now in the sixth decade of our life together.

Jane and I met on a Sunday evening at the Greyhound Bus Station in downtown Montgomery. We both were returning to Huntingdon from seeing old flames—back home in Linden for me and in Eastaboga for Jane. My friend Janice Wolf, traveling with me from Linden, introduced us, and we shared the cost of a taxi back to the dorms where we lived. Little did we know that our meeting would shape our lives over the next half century! I fell head over heels in love with Jane. One of my favorite early memories was riding a bicycle built for two with her out into the country, having a picnic and sharing our first kiss in a pasture where the Alabama Shakespeare Festival's theater now stands. There, surrounded by Jersey cows, we experienced the high drama of falling in love.

I am never sure about people who talk about two people being destined for each other because there are far too many ifs, ands, buts, and maybes in life, but for Jane and me, our separate lives had experienced events that groomed us for each other. Our parents were middle-class Methodists from the Deep South who believed in their children growing up in the faith of the church. Sunday was a holy day, and you went to church in the morning and evening. Jane's parents took her and her older sister, Nancy, to services at the rural congregation of Craig Memorial Methodist Church located just outside Anniston, Alabama. My parents had me and my older brother, Jimmy, in church every Sunday in Linden, Alabama. We were both taught early on to respect all people, to tell the truth, and to treat others as we wanted to be treated. Jane and I both loved being with people, loved learning, and loved the church. We were well prepared for each other well before we came together, but after our bus station meeting in 1961, it was but a matter of *when* we would marry, not *if* we would marry.

In the summer of 1962, after my freshman year and Jane's sophomore year, we were married, and in the next spring, on March 22, 1963, came our first daughter, Elizabeth Ann. There we were, nineteen and twenty years old, married and parents. It wasn't the smartest plan, but we both have always done what we felt was God's will for our lives, and we claimed opportunities when they presented themselves to us. Jane and

I would grow up together in the 1960s, and our lives would begin to blend. We had separate personalities, but through the years, we have truly become one in our commitments, values, hopes, and dreams. Our common love of God and shared desire to make a difference in the world through our service to others has truly shaped our lives.

One of the wonderful early memories of our shared commitment to serving God was a night in the first year of our marriage when we went to Dexter Avenue Methodist Church to hear Dr. E. Stanley Jones preach. He spoke to a packed house for well over an hour and a half. At the time, Jane was about eight months pregnant with Ann. At the end of a long sermon in which both Jane and I were spellbound, Dr. Jones made a prayerful plea for people to go to India as missionaries. As he prayed, he asked those who were willing to go to stand up. I felt a stirring beside me and opened my eyes to see Jane on her feet. As I rose to stand beside her, I thought, *"Thank you, God, for allowing me to be married to the most wonderful, most dedicated person I have ever known, but*

I'm not sure that going to India is one of our better decisions."

God didn't open that door, but we have gone together wherever he did lead us over the years. It was the first time but not the last time that we would pray together John Wesley's Covenant Prayer:

> I am no longer my own but yours,
> Put me to what you will.
> Put me to doing! Put me to suffering.
> Let me be employed for you,
>   or laid aside for you,
> Let me be full, let me be empty,
> Let me have all things, let me have nothing:
> I freely and wholeheartedly yield all things
>   to Your pleasure and disposal.
> And now glorious and blessed God,
> Father, Son, and Holy Spirit,
> You are mine and I am yours. So be it. And this covenant now made on earth, let it be satisfied in Heaven.
> Amen.

A Life Story

The 1960s was a time of great change for the nation and for our new family. We would live in more places in that decade than in the rest of our entire lives. We started out in the dorms at Huntingdon. After marrying we lived in a second-floor apartment next to the fire station across from the college and then moved up by moving downstairs in the same apartment building, which meant we were closer to the outside clothesline where we hung diapers day and night. Jane met me on the steps of that home with the news that President John F. Kennedy had been shot. In our first official appointment in 1962, we moved into a new parsonage in Bermuda, Alabama ,a small community outside Monroeville, Alabama. Next came the parsonage home in Boylston on the outskirts of Montgomery, followed by a basement apartment and a lovely little cottage during my graduate school years at Emory University. In 1967, my first appointment out of seminary took us to a run-down apartment in Union Springs, Alabama. Two years later we moved to Mobile, appointed to Dauphin Way United Methodist

Church, and moved into an old but spacious home in the Macy Place neighborhood. From that point, we would live in only six other homes. From the Macy Place home, we would move to the Clanton Parsonage in the church yard in 1974 and in 1978 into the new parsonage with breathtaking sunsets over Yellow Leaf Road on the outskirts of town. In 1979, we moved into the Marianna parsonage, and in 1984, we settled into Pensacola First Church's old parsonage on Tanglewood Drive. In 1986, we purchased our first home on Montalvo Drive and would live there for twenty years until we moved into our dream cottage on Pensacola Bay in 2006. We were so blessed to have many houses that quickly became sacred homes filled with warm laughter and love.

The early 1960s were a busy time, and it was evident that the Old South was crumbling at long last. Black Americans were claiming their place under the forceful, nonviolent ways of Rev. Martin Luther King Jr., Rev. Ralph David Abernathy, and John Lewis. Reverend Abernathy (1926-1990) was born in Marengo County, about ten miles outside of my hometown of Linden. Rev. Abernathy, who led protest demonstrations all over the nation, focused on the cities of St. Augustine, Albany, Atlanta, Memphis, Chicago, Montgomery, and Selma. These were cities that had strong local support for the cause of change. He never scheduled a protest in his hometown of Linden.

However, the KKK did have demonstrations in Linden. Although these demonstrations were meant to be scary, with men in their white robes and masks, as a teenager I was not intimidated. During one KKK march, my friends and I actually took a screwdriver and popped the little red marbles out of the headlights of their fancy cars as these men marched down the main street of town. I still have some of those red marbles today and they remind me of those crazy times, with those idiots desperately trying to preserve a terrible way of life in the deep South that was destined to end.

Abernathy was thirty-nine years old when he started marching with King and Lewis and hundreds of others from Selma to Montgomery across the Edmund Pettus Bridge on March 21, 1965. By the time I enrolled at Huntingdon, he had been the pastor of the First Baptist Church of Montgomery for ten years. Lewis was born on a farm just outside of Selma toward Troy and was twenty-five years old at the time of the march. He would later become one of the outstanding U.S. Congressional leaders for change in the entire nation.

Iona Johnson and I were both in Montgomery during the Selma march, both in our early twenties, but we were still living parallel lives. Neither of us participated in the march. Iona told me that she didn't march because she was afraid. I didn't participate because I had decided I needed to choose a different way to make my contribution to the demand for change in race relations. At the time, I was serving as a student pastor at Boylston Methodist Church. A week before the march, Bishop Kenneth Goodson called an evening meeting in a downtown hotel of all the Methodist ministers serving churches in the area and encouraged us to not participate in the march. He urged us to be friendly and open to the Black marchers and other visitors who might come to our churches during those tense days, telling us, "We will have to serve as a peaceful force for good after the march." Even today I see my ministry as a peaceful force for good. I listened to our bishop and obeyed his instructions. It was not the last time I would be obedient to the instructions of our bishop but would look back thinking I should have listened to the voice within rather than the voice of human authority.

My studies as a history major at Huntingdon had changed my sensitivity and awareness of the plight of Black citizens and helped me develop a more open view of the need for change in my homeland. Many voices influenced my decisions in those formative years, and sometimes it was hard to determine the truth of what was right or wrong to do as a young minister. I prayed for those who marched to Montgomery and for the growing movement to bring change. Later, with the perspective of the years, I would wonder about my decision not to be more active in the Selma march. It was indeed a missed opportunity to be part of a significant moment in the dynamic history of the 1960s.

While at Emory, I heard Reverend King speak in a Black church in Atlanta and was greatly moved. It was a time when Malcom X was promoting Black Power, and Reverend King spoke to his congregants about the need for Green Power, which was all about getting good jobs and demanding in nonviolent ways a fair, living wage for all Americans. America owes a great debt to Reverend King, Reverend Abernathy, and other Black leaders in the Southern Christian Leadership Conference for promoting nonviolent protest. Their commitment to peace brought about change in an explosive era in America's history and saved the Old South from a blood bath.

It's strange how I grew up beside so many outstanding Black leaders but never really knew them or their families. We lived parallel lives, separate but never equal, while a revolution was brewing in the kettle of life in America. I feel a deep gratitude for their courage, faith, and service but also sadness. There I was in Montgomery, starting a family and a career in the church, but I never sat down with them to get to know them or talk about their vision. What a missed opportunity.

As I think back on other missed opportunities during those years of segregation, I recall an interesting formative experience that crossed the line between Black and white. When I turned nineteen years old in the spring of 1961, I graduated from Linden High School, the only all-white school in our county. As the president of the student government association, I was asked to open the graduation ceremony with a devotion. I cannot for the life of me remember which teacher placed in my hands a poem and insisted that I perform a recitation of James Weldon Johnson's poem "The Creation." There I was, a white kid standing before an all-white audience and reciting a poem by a Black man from Jacksonville, Florida, which opened, "And God stepped out on space/And he looked around and said: I'm lonely/I'll make me a world." I didn't know, and I suspect that not a single person in that audience of forty-nine students and another 150 parents and family members had a clue that it was a poem by a Black man expressing new hopes for a new day.

I later discovered that Johnson is famous for many wonderful poems. Two that have always stood out to me are "Lift Every Voice and Sing," which was written in 1900 and today is known as the Black National Anthem, and "Oh Southland," which Johnson penned in 1907.

Lift Every Voice and Sing

Lift every voice and sing,
'Til Earth and Heaven ring,
Ring with the harmonies of Liberty;
Let our rejoicing rise
High as the listening skies,
Let it resound loud as the rolling sea.
Sing a song full of the faith
   that the dark past has taught us,
Sing a song full of the hope
   that the present has brought us;
Facing the rising sun of our new day begun,

Let us march on 'til victory is won.
Stony the road we trod,
Bitter the chastening rod,
Felt in the days when hope unborn had died;
Yet with a steady beat,
Have not our weary feet
Come to the place for which our fathers sighed?
We have come over a way
  that with tears has been watered,
We have come, treading our path
  through the blood of the slaughtered,
Out from the gloomy past,
'Til now we stand at last
Where the white gleam of our bright star is cast.
God of our weary years,
God of our silent tears,
Thou who has brought us thus far on the way;
Thou who has by Thy might
Led us into the light,
Keep us forever in the path, we pray.
Lest our feet stray from the places, our God,
where we met Thee,

our hearts drunk with the wine of the world,
we forget Thee;
Shadowed beneath Thy hand,
May we forever stand,
True to our God,
True to our native land.

O Southland!

O Southland! O Southland!
Have you not heard the call,
The trumpet blown, the word made known
To the nations, one and all?
The watchword, the hope-word,
Salvation's present plan?
A gospel new, for all--for you:
Man shall be saved by man.

O Southland! O Southland!
Do you not hear to-day
The mighty beat of onward feet,
 And know you not their way?

A Life Story

'Tis forward, 'tis upward,
On to the fair white arch
Of Freedom's dome, and there is room
For each man who would march.

O Southland, fair Southland!
Then why do you still cling
To an idle age and a musty page,
To a dead and useless thing?
'Tis springtime! 'Tis work-time!
The world is young again!
And God's above, and God is love,
And men are only men.

O Southland! my Southland!
O birthland! do not shirk
The toilsome task, nor respite ask,
But gird you for the work.
Remember, remember
That weakness stalks in pride;
That he is strong who helps along
The faint one at his side.

It is astounding what God can do with people, whether they are white or black or rich or poor. Jane and I believed this wholeheartedly, and we were hopeful about the future as we settled in Atlanta and pursued graduate degrees. She worked on a master's degree in math at Emory University and took a job teaching math in an interracial high school in the East Lake neighborhood of Decatur, Georgia. I worked as an oxygen therapist at Grady Hospital on night shifts and as a part time youth pastor at Grace United Methodist Church while also attending Candler School of Theology. We worked long hours to pay the bills and put food on the table, and while there was little time for play, we did enjoy free concerts, city life, and the beautiful parks where we would play with Ann. One of our favorite pastimes was driving out to the hill overlooking Hartsfield International Airport and watching all the planes landing and taking off in the early evening light. There were no airports in Linden, so this was an amazing scene for two county kids from Alabama.

One of the most devastating experiences of those years was the death of Jane's dad, Woody Strange, who died March 12, 1966, at the age of 53. A wonderful Christian man, he was a smoker and died from cardiac arrest. I have, ever since his loss, hated smoking and the price so many pay at the hands of this self-inflicted disease. Jane's mother, Elizabeth Montgomery Strange, was a kind and caring Christian woman who would live for another forty years without the love of her life, but would continue to share love with her children and community.

During those years in Atlanta, I continued to have my eyes opened about the presence of racial prejudice within the Methodist Church. One of my friends in seminary was also the only Black student at Candler School of Theology at that time. He would ride with us on Sunday morning and attend Sunday School and worship at Grace Church until a very strange thing happened. The senior pastor asked me to visit with him in his office, and during our talk, he asked that I not bring my Black friend back to church. The reason he gave was that the church was in the middle of a big financial campaign for a new building and the timing was just not ideal. I was obedient to his request but knew in my heart that it was just not right. I understood racism because in my early, formative years I had grown up with the ignorance and resentment that informs prejudice. Because of my education, however, I could no longer hold on to the shortsighted, judgmental ways of racism. I had changed, but I lived in a society that had not. Parts of Atlanta were burning in those days, and in my heart, I, too, had a simmering fire of anger about what was happening.

The publishing of the book "The Feminine Mystique" by Betty Friedan in 1963 announced a call to feminism and raised awareness of the fight for gender equality. There was only one woman in my seminary class at the Candler School of Theology in the 1960s where today more than 50 percent of the current ministerial students and medical and law students are female. When I finally became the Senior Minister of a local church in 1973, I would never again serve a church in which I did not place on our staff a female minister.

In 1964, after a long struggle that climaxed with choking off a record three-month filibuster led by Southern Democrats in the U.S. Senate, President Lyndon B. Johnson signed the Civil Rights Act. The sweeping measure outlawed racial discrimination in restaurants, theaters, hotels, and other public accommodations. It also empowered the federal government to end segregation in public places such as schools and hospitals. Thanks to an opponent's strategic blunder, the law banned discrimination in employment based on sex as well as race. Rep. Howard Smith, a Democrat from Virginia, inserted the gender issue into the legislative bill, hoping to garner enough anti-feminist votes to kill it entirely. But when the bill passed, Smith's miscalculation ensured that both Blacks and women would thenceforth be protected by federal law. Times were a-changing in the 1960s.

Jane and I were moving around, learning, making commitments, and dealing as best we could with the reality of parenting our two girls. Along the way, we encountered the joys and sadness of a changing world, mingled with personal sacrifices demanded of those who seek to be servants of God. There was in our minds and hearts a naïve confidence that we could change things and make the world a better place. While the 1960s were the beginning of great and marvelous years, it was also an era of challenge, change, pain, and loss.

When I approached the completion of my seminary studies, Bishop Goodson and Montgomery District Superintendent Powers McCleod came to Atlanta and invited me to return to the Alabama-West Florida Conference. I had little motivation to return to the Deep South of my roots to preach a somewhat liberal, social gospel that I was slanting toward in my seminary studies. This slant was not always appreciated in the white churches. Bishop Goodson spoke of the challenge of preaching and leading congregations in an era of transition and the need for young men to return to Alabama and serve the causes of Christ. At the time I was considering going into some professorship in a college or into a military chaplaincy or something else, but not returning to Alabama. Bishop Goodson was passionate in recruiting young men who saw their ministry including the battle for racial justice. He was a forceful and effective preacher who had been elected a bishop when he was fifty-one years old. He would guide both the North Alabama and Alabama-West Florida conferences to eliminate the racial division created by the old Central Jurisdiction, and he was recruiting young ministers to join him in bringing about a day of at least structural unity of Black and white ministers.

It was McCleod who spoke frankly with fire in his eyes, telling me, "You can run from this if you want to, but Christ needs people like you to come back home and help us get through this revolution and be true to the Way of Christ where people of all races are respected."

They wanted us to move to Union Springs, Alabama, and they both described it as the most historic appointment in all of Methodism. What happened in the Union Springs Church was that the congregation had divided on racial attitudes and the liberal affirmative positions and actions of the United Methodist Church. The Alabama State Legislature had passed a bill called the Dumas Act, which allowed a local congregation of any church denomination to pull out of that denomination with a majority vote and claim the properties for the local church. Of course, the United Methodist Church properties are, by constitutional church law, held in trust for the ministry of the denomination, and the conference would not allow this to happen. In Alabama in the 1960s, however, it did happen in Union Springs, Alabama, and the United Methodist Church was thrown out and a Southern Methodist Church was organized in the same properties and claimed on the basis of the Dumas Act. The conference went to court to reclaim the property, but the problem was that it was the 1960s and Gov. George Wallace's brother, Jack Wallace, was the Circuit Judge who heard the case and decided against the United Methodist Church and gave the property to the local majority. There were twenty-two members, primarily United Methodist Women who were loyal to the United Methodist Church and some of their families, in the Union Springs Church who wanted to stay faithful to our denomination. They had organized and were meeting in the basement of the public library and waiting for a new minister to arrive.

It was into this transition time that Bishop Goodson appointed me to go and serve. I was young, fired up, and ready to charge forward into some kind of battle, no matter what. The fact that the bishop thought that I was up to the job fed my ego, so I was ready to go. In reality, I was fresh out of seminary, married with a three-year-old daughter, and going into a very uncertain situation that provided a $1,550.00 annual salary. It was the kind of thing that illustrated what stupid and dumb looks like up close and personal.

In the summer of 1967, we packed up all our worldly possessions into a small U-Haul truck and moved to Union Springs. One of the joys was that as we were moving into Bullock County, there was another young couple also beginning a similar career move who were no strangers to us.

Joe Hendrickson was the new high school football coach, and he and his wife, Janice, and their first child, Eve, moved in just down the street. Not only had I known Janice since kindergarten, but she was also the person who had introduced me to Jane. She and Joe were new to the community, they were our friends, and they were Methodists! They were our first new members in the church of twenty people who met in the basement of the city library. My ministry primarily consisted of trying to speak a word of peace and unity to a radically divided community. It was a message that was not always appreciated.

On one dismal night in early April, as I was approaching my twenty-sixth birthday and speaking at a small Methodist Church Men's Club dinner in a church just outside of Troy, Alabama, someone at the end of the meeting announced the news that Martin Luther King Jr. had been killed in Memphis. The whites-only meeting broke into rousing applause. I was sick to my stomach and was, in that moment, changed forever and resolved to get off the sidelines and become involved in the movement of racial change.

The very next week I met with Annie Mae Turner, a teacher in Union Springs and a member of our church, and we started an organization that created a day care program for the children who lived in a Black housing project in Bullock County. The goal was to help young mothers make a living and provide for the education and safety of their young children who would later take over and be leaders in the Alabama of the future. It was a small act of trying to make a difference and the way I would choose to bring about change in the communities where I would serve for the next half-century.

I became very intentional about reaching out to the Black citizens of our small county seat and would often be invited to preach at their churches. One Wednesday evening as I was walking out of the house to preach at a local Black Baptist church, our five-year-old daughter, Ann, asked where I was going. I said, "To the Black Baptist Church." She responded, "To the Baptist Church? Why?"

Ann was fine with it being a Black church, but she wasn't so sure about it being *Baptist*. She has, from those days to this day, always been open and accepting of people of all races, but she's fiercely loyal to her Methodist roots. A child of my own heart.

Our second daughter, Rebecca, was born into our family in May 1968 and what joy that brought in the early, hard times of our ministerial life in Union Springs. When she was only a year old, Puff, a cockapoo, would also join our family and be with us for the first eleven years of Rebecca's life. What joy and blessings to have a new baby and a loving pet, both of whom offered to us unconditional love. Puff lived with us for a full decade and was buried beside my parent's riverside cabin on Lay Lake on the Coosa River in central Alabama. Rebecca would go on to become a citizen of the world through her studies at Birmingham Southern College, the University of Alabama Law School, the London School of Economics, and then her career as a lawyer and reinsurance executive in Bermuda.

In the years that followed, our daughters would be a part of our lives and convictions and grow into unique individuals while also being PKs (preacher's kids). Ann and Rebecca would enjoy the privilege of travel and meeting the best of people. They would be influenced by Helen Parish, a Christian educator at Clanton as well as many other great servants of the church. Ann would feel the hardships of our convictions about the need for integration of schools as she started school in Mobile and then finished high school in Clanton. She would develop her love for art, animals, and life. Rebecca would grow in laughter, fun, and academic success through colleges and universities that launched her bravely and successfully into an international arena of the insurance industry and the sport of sailing.

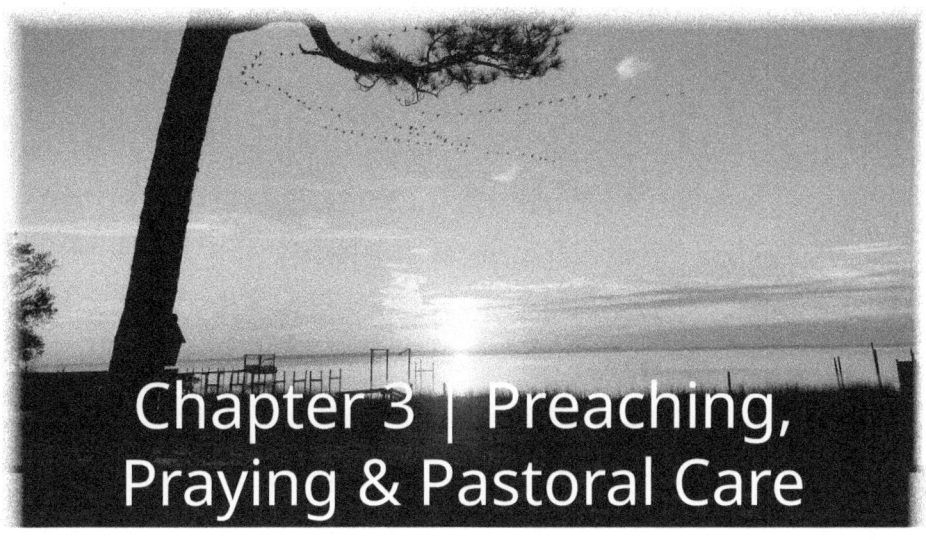

Chapter 3 | Preaching, Praying & Pastoral Care

1970-1980

When the 1970s dawned, Jane and the girls and I lived in Mobile, where I was an associate minister at the Dauphin Way church. As I was growing and learning what it meant to be a pastor in the Deep South in a time of immense social change, Jane became a stay-at-home mom to provide security and support for Ann and Rebecca.

At Dauphin Way, I was privileged to work under the guidance and tutorship of Joel McDavid and Steve Dill, my senior ministers. Joel would go on to be a Bishop in the United Methodist Church, and Steve would serve at Dauphin Way the rest of his life, showing me the beauty and effectiveness of a long-term pastorate to an entire city. Their strong leadership in the church gave me some latitude for creativity because I did not carry the entire responsibility for the local ministry.

During this time, I was able to work in youth ministry and was privileged to organize a chapter of the Wesley Foundation at the fast-growing University of South Alabama. It was there I became aware that many young women facing problem pregnancies were suffering at the hands of so-called doctors in second-rate, illegal medical clinics. Although they had turned to these places for help, they often emerged worse off and dealing with challenging medical conditions. In 1973, the U.S. Supreme Court's ruling on *Roe V. Wade* had legalized abortion in America, but there were virtually no safe or legitimate medical facilities in the state of Alabama that offered these services. In response, I joined a couple of other young ministers in connecting with the Clergy Consultation Service, a national organization that offered free clergy counseling to women and girls facing problem pregnancies. From an advertised telephone answering service, we would return calls to desperate young women, and on the days when I would be on call, I would meet with them and explore various options that included homes for unwed mothers, adoption, and abortion.

In those years, the only place that we could refer women to for safe abortions was a hospital in New York City. I often thought of these young, poor, and frightened girls and women who would travel to New York for these services. What courage they had to take charge of their broken lives and make these hard choices. The CCS offered these young women counseling in a nonjudgmental environment, and we referred them to trustworthy places where they could find help. We also prayed with them to follow God's will for their lives. My chief aim was to offer hope and guidance to desperate young women trying to make grown-up decisions with very little information and even less support. Instead of being guided by a single rigid ideology, I strived to look at these women as individuals who were beloved by God and facing hugely difficult circumstances.

I have always approached life's dilemmas with the understanding that often there is no right or wrong choice. At those times, I have tried to choose my path prayerfully and actively seeking God's help, and I believe the faith we exhibit in those moments has the power to shape the rest of our lives. I have believed all my life that God offers a way to a better tomorrow when we seek his way for our individual journey. As part of the CCS, I was dealing with difficult decisions and walking a fine line of moral responsibility while also trying to live a compassionate, caring life helping the poor and vulnerable. These were young women, often victims of abuse, who were desperate for someone to hold their hands and pray with them as they made momentous life decisions.

Abortion is such a sacred, holy decision because it involves the lives of so many people. The decision must not be made by the government or a family majority vote, but by the expectant mother with the best medical and spiritual advice she can find. Usually, these young women I met with were pregnant as a result of sexual abuse or rape rather than a loving relationship. When this happens, hard decisions have to be made about one's future life and the life of the developing fetus. That decision must be made in the mind and heart of one individual, the female mother.

The weight of that ministry—and the many questions it prompted me to ask myself—was great, and I often sought solace in the beautiful Chancel Window inside the sanctuary at Dauphin Way. On Sundays, I would sit quietly in my associate minister's role and gaze at the sparkling stained glass window, which had been designed by the Willet Stained Glass Studios of Philadelphia and installed in 1957. Resurrection was the focal point of the window but what always captured my attention was the emphasis on the acts of mercy highlighted by Jesus in Matthew 25:31-46, RSV:

> "For I was hungry and you gave me food; I was thirsty and you gave me drink; I was a stranger, and you welcomed me; I was naked, and you clothed me; I was sick, and you visited me; I was in prison, and you came to me. . . . Truly, I say to you as you did it to one of the least of these my brethren, you did it to me."

Surrounding the Resurrected Jesus in that towering window was a host of faithful saints over the ages. Nearest the Christ figure were the disciples of his own day with other outstanding Christian leaders down through the ages. There was Paul, John, and Stephen but also Francis of Assisi (1182-1226), the founder of the Franciscan Order who was born into a life of privilege but renounced his wealth to live a life of poverty; Albert Schweitzer (1875-1965), philosopher, musician, and medical missionary; Walter Rauschenbusch (1861-1918), a Baptist minister known as the father of the Social Gospel; Toyohiko Kagawa (1888-1960), a Presbyterian minister and social worker for the people of Japan; Anselm of Canterbury (1033-1109), a Benedictine monk who became Archbishop of Canterbury; Peter Abelard (1079-1142), a French monk and poet who was one of the great minds of the twelfth century; Columba (512-597), an Irish missionary to Scotland who founded the monasteries at Derry and Durrow and on the Isle of Iona in Scotland; Martin Niemöller (1892-1984), a German submarine commander in World War I who later became a minister and led the resistance to Adolph Hitler; John Wesley (1703-1791), the founder of Methodism who preached, "Do all the good you can for as many as you can for as long as you can." Also depicted in the window was Francis Asbury (1745-1816), who was first sent by Wesley to establish American Methodism in 1771 when he was twenty-six years old.

I was the same age as I sat in that pew praying and seeking to understand my role in the great scheme of Christ's ministry in an age of social change. My mind often wandered to the way they had put their faith into action and devoted their very lives to the betterment of others. Through the years, I have sought to call on God's people to be faithful servants who reach out caring hands to those in great need. The desire to reach across "The Ditches" that separate the rich and the poor would fundamentally shape my ministry for years to come.

In fact, social justice was far more than an academic notion for our family. In the early 1970s, it was a reality we saw play out from day to day. At this time, federal courts were still trying to enforce integration and create some kind of racial balance in the public schools across Mobile County. For Ann, who was in elementary school, this meant moving between three different schools in two years. Jane and I believed in supporting the public schools rather than running to the all-white private schools, and we were encouraged by Joel McDavid, our senior minister, to keep that commitment. It was difficult to see our child pay the price for our moral convictions. Jane would often cry as she sent Ann off to school, knowing the confusion and difficulty of all the uncertainty she would face.

By 1973, our war-weary nation had brought an end to the Vietnam War, a ten-year conflict with a price tag of 57,000 young soldiers dead and many more injured mentally and physically. In August 1974, President Richard Nixon finally left the White House amid the Watergate scandal. I remember becoming aware of a creative fundraising campaign at Emory University in those years, which asked, "Can anyone over thirty be trusted?" It was a question that would haunt our nation and my attitude toward elected government and church leaders for many years. It just seemed like elected officials were more interested in keeping things as they were, rather than inviting change to make things as they ought to be.

During my time at Dauphin Way, through Steve Dill's interest in supporting the World Council of Churches, I became the chairman of the Conference Committee on Ecumenical Affairs, and I was privileged to represent the Alabama-West Florida Conference at international conferences in England and Brazil. We often had marvelous speakers out of those encounters come to the Dauphin Way Church to speak to the congregation. I was in a unique position as the associate minister to entertain them and look after them while they were visiting in Mobile, and one of the finest I came to know was George Buttrick, a scholar, pastor, and outstanding preacher. He had succeeded Henry Sloane Coffin as the minister of Madison Avenue Presbyterian

Church in New York City and served there for twenty-eight years. Later in his retirement years he taught homiletics at Garrett Seminary and Louisville Southern Baptist Seminary and served as the editor of *The Interpreter's Bible,* which became a basic guide for most ministers in their Bible studies in the latter part of the twentieth century. Buttrick published twelve books, but only one book of sermons, *Sermons Preached in a University Church.* He was very hesitant about publishing these sermons, for three reasons that he shares in the book's preface. First, he asserted, the preacher writes for the ear and must now rewrite for the eye. Secondly, the sermon is an "I-thou" transaction in that the congregation makes the sermon almost as much as the preacher. Third, a sermon is a part of worship and is itself a worship experience. "Remove the prayer-worship, the brooding of the Spirit on the worshiping congregation, and how much of the sermon is left?" Buttrick's insight and delightful spirit would guide my thoughts and ministry style for years. Ultimately it would shape the direction of my doctoral studies.

On a side note, I would correspond with Buttrick when he was in his late seventies and early eighties. He died in his mid-eighties, and his wonderful wife, Agnes, stayed close to him during his final years and would often correct him or help him complete a sentence. She served as his editor-in-chief for all of his works, which he said authenticated the old saying, "Behind every good man is a good woman telling him what to do." I have thought of their beautiful relationship often over the years and especially on Sunday mornings as I left to go to the church and Jane would walk me to the car and ask, "What are you preaching on today?" I would tell her in a faltering speech what I had planned to say. Keep in mind this was after a month of preparation, a week of writing, and two days of vocalizing the sermon in the shower and outside in the backyard. And in a split second, Jane would say to me, off the cuff, "You might want to think about …" More times than not, she would cut to the heart of what needed to be said, saving an entire congregation from my ramblings. Jane wasn't behind me telling me what to do, but she was certainly standing firmly by my side, offering gentle suggestions to make my sermons look unbelievably polished.

While living in Mobile, from 1970 to 1974, we enjoyed having my brother, Jimmy, and sister-in-law, GaNelle, and their girls, nearby for the first time since growing up in Linden. Jimmy consistently set new heights in athletic achievements during our high school years, and I was five years behind him but always trying to measure up to him and his standards. In the 1970s, he advanced in his profession as an insurance agent with Nationwide and later built a successful State Farm office in the Germantown community of Memphis. In the Mobile years, Jimmy gave his time every Sunday night, working with the Mobile Inner-City Mission and helping tutor and coach young Black students who had the difficult task of growing up in beleaguered downtown neighborhoods. In Memphis, there were several young

Black female basketball players that were a part of Jimmy's Germantown family. They sat with us in the family section of the church and cried with us over his great loss when he died at the age of fifty-nine from cancer. Through the years, he and I had tried in our own ways to fight against racism's stain on the lives of those children who grew up on the other side of the ditch from our privileged lives.

Another of the lasting memories of the Mobile years were the wonderful people that I came to know and enjoy. Like Ruth Penton, the Conference Youth Director, and Nina Reaves of the North Alabama Conference, whom I joined to lead citizenship tours for teenagers to visit Washington D.C. and the United Nations in New York. We met with Henry Kissinger, Yasser Arafat, and Desmond Tutu in the early years of their lives as they were trying to promote world peace and unity. I often pray for peace and unity among the peoples of the world, and like racial harmony, it seems to be an elusive goal. It doesn't mean I don't continue to long for these hopes to be fulfilled, but today's news indicates they are hopes yet to be realized.

Our family moved to Clanton, Alabama in 1974 where I served as the pastor of the church my father grew up in as a child and young adult. These were meaningful years for our family as Jane taught math in the community of Maplesville, Alabama and I went back to graduate school to complete my doctorate of ministry at Emory as she finished her master's in counseling at the University of Montevallo.

Perhaps the most unusual gift of these years was that after a successful career with the Alabama Power Company and as a community leader in Linden, my father retired. Starting a new chapter in their life, my parents moved back to their ancestral home territory in Chilton County, where both had grown up, met, married, and started their family. I was, during these years, their son and their pastor. They were such good parents over the years as they had always told me what they thought and cautioned me when I was off base and needed guidance. Ultimately, they gave me enough freedom to become my own person and cheered me on in so many ways. No person could have been more fortunate than I had been to have them as my parents.

The Clanton years became a productive time in our life as Jane and I were once again students and parents of growing girls. Ann and Rebecca enjoyed having Tennessee Walking Horses, which we rode in the country, and water skiing on the Coosa River at my parent's riverside cottage. Rebecca would start school, and Ann would graduate from high school in Clanton, which meant spending her senior year with my parents after we had moved on to our next appointment in Marianna, Florida. Ann remembers that her "Pop" would say to her, "You can sit there and cry as long as you want to, but eventually you are going to have to suck it up and get up and do something." It was a life lesson my father had learned early and one he had passed on to his two sons and his grandchildren.

It was during these Clanton years that I began to focus on "The Three Ps" of my calling:

Preaching, Praying, and Pastoral Care. These are all active verbs, and I believe that the churches I have served during this time grew not because of my great wisdom or ability, but because I worked hard and communicated a genuine caring spirit.

I learned that preaching is a mystical experience where the minister looks back through our sacred literature to our old faith stories and applies the discovered truths of Holy Scripture to the life experiences of today. I don't believe that in today's world that people come to church to hear an all-knowing, educated minister teach them something. They come with the broken pieces of their lives in their hands and want help putting things together again. They come seeking a comforting and affirming word that will help them make sense of the chaos found in a world out of control.

I have been guided during the last thirty years of my ministry by the lectionary selections of the scriptures, which year after year and Sunday after Sunday keeps the minister and the church focused on the great themes of the Christian faith. I have viewed my preaching not as a task of teaching, but as a pastoral function. Looking back over the years, I recall a number of sermons or favorite messages based on Paul's affirmation, "I can do all things through Christ who strengthens me," and Jesus's affirmations in John 14:14, "I will do whatever you ask in my name," and Mark 11:24, "Whatever you ask for in prayer, believe that you have received it and it will be yours." People seem to listen more carefully when we communicate not what we know but that we understand their pain, that we care, and that there is hope.

My doctoral dissertation, which resulted in my doctorate of ministry in 1978, was entitled, "Developing New Capacities for Hearing the Word in the Preaching Event." In this rather lengthy document, I viewed the preaching experiences of the lectionary themes as far more than merely a history lesson of the central truths of salvation history. I wrote in my dissertation: "The preaching event served as an integrating function for believers as it offered a model for the organization of their individual religious experiences into a meaningful whole. Viewed pastorally, the Church Year becomes a bridge between our historical/rational background and the existential/mystical side of our life experiences."

Chapter 4 | The Florida Years

1980-2006

On a hot June day in 1980, we cried as our family pulled out of my mom and dad's driveway, leaving Clanton and heading to Marianna, Florida. It was a move that would focus our life and ministry in Northwest Florida for the next four decades. We left with my parents waving to us from their home, but as always, I knew that we would be in their prayers and concerns as we ventured into new territory. In my experience, parents worry about their children. You cannot simply move away from the love and concern of a parent.

By this time, Jane had completed her master's degree in educational counseling, and as we established our life in Florida, she became a leader for children's issues in the local communities where we lived as well as in the state political arena. During our Marianna years, she would help organize The Greenwood Child Development Center, a school for children who were delayed or developmentally challenged, and when we moved to Pensacola, she worked in the Development Evaluation and Intervention Program linked with the Sacred Heart Health System for fifteen years until she retired to care for our mothers, who would move to Pensacola to be near us during their final years. Jane's mother, Lib, was ninety-one years old when she died in Jane's arms at Wesley Haven Villa on May 15, 2006. My mother, Gladys, would die at The Haven nursing home when she was 92.

We lived and served in Marianna from June 1980 to August 1984. These were good years for our family, and there were many opportunities for me to serve in the ministries of the Alabama-West Florida Conference. I was privileged to be chairman of the Conference Board of Education, the Council on Ministries, and later the most challenging job of chairman of the Board of Ordained Ministry. These roles helped me decide that I did not want to pursue the administrative jobs of District Superintendent or Bishop as my gifts were not in managing personnel. There were others who liked to do those kinds of things but not me. I would often say about the tasks of ministry: "I preach and teach and counsel and visit the sick and reach out to new members for free, but the church pays me to run the staff."

At some point during these years, I was riding with my friend Herb Sadler to some church meeting, and we were discussing our friends, Karl Stegall, David Chunn, and Jimmy Carpenter, all of whom had grown up in the Black Belt area of West Alabama. There we were, all serving on various boards and committees within the Alabama-West Florida Conference, and we laughed together, recognizing that we could no longer gripe about the "sorry leadership" because now we were it! This sea change made us realize that the leadership of any organization was probably doing its best to be true to its mission.

Two of my most cherished gifts from the Marianna years were the friendships I cultivated with two Circuit Judges—Judge Robert McCrary and Judge John Roberts. McCrary was a faithful church member and for a period served as the Chairman of the Finance and Administration Committee of the Alabama-West Florida Conference. Judge McCrary presided over the trial of Clarence Gideon, a poor man in Panama City who could not afford a lawyer and was denied a court-appointed attorney. He was convicted and sentenced to prison in 1961, but he appealed his case, which ultimately led to the U.S. Supreme Court ruling in *Gideon v. Wainwright* that adequate legal representation is a fundamental right of those who cannot afford a lawyer and that indigent criminal defendants in the U. S. courts will be provided representation at the state's expense. The ruling led to the expansion of the public defender systems in Florida and beyond.

One of the old tales that Judge McCrary told on himself was that because he had to run for the judgeship, he would often go into a large gathering of people, whether at church or a political gathering, and work the room from left to right, shaking hands and asking folks about their family, farm or whatever. One time he asked a fellow, "How's your mother?" The man responded, "She died last year, Judge, but thank you for asking." He offered his condolences and continued to work the room. The problem was that he forgot where he had started shaking hands and came back to the same fellow, inquiring a second time about his mother—to which the man replied, "She's still dead Judge, still dead."

I would often go dove hunting with Judge McCrary, but one day that stopped. We had killed several birds, and I brought them home for supper. As I was dressing them, I realized that our young daughter, Rebecca, had come outside to where the dead birds were stacked high and asked as she stroked their feathers, "Why did you do this?" And then I noticed big tears in her eyes. That was the last day I ever went hunting, and although I still have my old rusty shotgun, I have not fired it for years and don't plan to ever kill anything again.

With our schooling days completed, and both of us working, there was a little more time and money to be had, so we began to do some traveling to explore the world. Having lived most of our lives within driving distance of the central part of Alabama, we discovered that we loved to travel and experience new places and all the diverse people who live in this global village. We started with a trip to the Middle East in 1972 and then one to Europe in 1974. My parents and several church friends traveled with us when I was but twenty-eight years old. Jane and I often laugh about that journey, during which we covered most of the capitals of Europe in seventeen days. There I was leading my parents and these other adults on a trip to Europe when I had never been farther than Alabama and Northwest Florida. We would return from those early trips and over the years we would go again and again. There were multiple trips to parts of Europe and focused, return trips to parts of the Holy Land as well as London, the Cotswolds, Oxford, and Stratford-upon-Avon.

I credit my European history courses at Huntingdon with motivating me to study these far-off places and then venture off to explore them. That wonderful liberal arts education opened my eyes to the wonder of travel and taught me the value of experiencing other people and places. Travel expanded my universe exponentially, and I began to envision a world where all people could experience the possibility of a complete life, where all could respect the rights of all, and all could pursue their dreams.

In 1984, I was appointed to First United Methodist Church in Downtown Pensacola. The move to Pensacola would be our last as I would spend more than half of my total of forty-four years of ministry in this final appointment. I can still remember how it felt when we drove over from Marianna and looked over a deteriorating downtown and several rundown church buildings. I became depressed and overwhelmed by what I saw and sensed, and it was Rebecca—who was moving away from high school friends and the security of a small home town into the eleventh grade at Washington High School—who said, "Daddy, you have made the decision to move on to Pensacola, stop worrying about it, move on, and make the best out of it." Her attitude and confidence would characterize much of her own success in high school, college, law school, and in the professional world.

We were fortunate at Pensacola First Church to ride the baby boom generation, who were returning to churches across America, seeking to give to their children what their parents had given to them. There were seventy-two million Americans born between 1947 and 1964, and the Pensacola First Church was well positioned to benefit from their growing interest in spirituality and security in the late 1980s and 1990s. With a new focus on children and parents with children, the church would grow by more than 59 percent in our membership over the twenty-three years I served there. Early on, the decision to add well trained staff members who would help focus our church on this target group was the secret to our growth. We had Bud Precise in educational ministries, Karen Evans in youth and children ministries, and Allen and Susan Pote and Rick and Heidi Branch in the music area. The church was also fortunate over the years to have very dedicated and well-trained associates like Larry Mosley, Alan Gantzhorn, Fred Zobel, Mark LaBranche, Kathy Atkins Allen, and Darryl Barrow. Their expertise and energy helped us reverse the trend of old downtown churches growing tired and dying and embark on a vibrant new beginning. There was also the crucial ingredient on our staff of Ginger Raines, who came to First Church as a volunteer and remained as my personal secretary for more than twenty years, outlasted me, and was an indispensable part of the church administration team.

I still remember with a smile the day soon after I added a children's time to the order of worship and invited all the children to come to the altar for a special message, and one lonely little girl came to the altar. Dr. J. B. Nichols, who had retired at

First Church after having a distinguished career of serving the church as both senior minister and associate minister, was present that day and suggested after the service that I might want to think about "renting some children" until we built up our numbers. Before long the children had to run down the aisle to find a place at the altar. We were immensely blessed by this new growth of young families and many children.

In 1993, the tenth year of ministry in Pensacola, there was increasing tension in our city between pro-life and pro-choice supporters, which eventually led to the murder of Dr. David Gunn, an obstetrics and gynecology doctor. The fatal shooting is believed to be the first documented murder of an abortion provider by an anti-abortion extremist in the United States. During this time of high tension, Mayor John Fogg came to me and asked if I would convene and mediate meetings of the leaders of the opposing positions to restore some semblance of peaceful sanity to our city. I agreed and hosted at the church several heated discussions between opponents and advocates of abortion while armed city policemen stood guard outside. Although we learned to listen to one another with respect and have civil, diplomatic conversations, our meetings brought no resolution.

Even to this day, that division persists and has grown particularly bitter since the Supreme Court overturned *Roe v. Wade* in June 2022, ending a woman's constitutional right to abortion. I find it terribly sad that these social issues continue to divide our human family. Those community meetings were not the first time that a minister from First Church would take the lead in Pensacola to bring opposing groups together for a peaceful resolution. In 1955, Nichols would convene Black and white leaders dealing with Civil Rights tensions, and in 1968, Dan Whitsett would bring together teachers and administrators to deal with public school issues.

There was a time when Methodist ministers would encourage parishioners to prepare for the next world, preaching that our purpose was to save people from the fires of hell and assure their place in heaven. I, on the other hand, have always felt that our purpose was not to prepare for the next life but to sound the alarm against evil and proclaim a way of life that helps establish the kingdom of heaven in the here and now. I have always believed that if we lived as Jesus taught, we would one day see fulfilled the words of the Lord's Prayer and that we would see God's kingdom and God's will established "on earth as it is in heaven." I do still carry a deep sadness that after all these years, there is still division in the human family and that we are still battling with fascism, terrorism, communism, racism, sexism and so much more. We have fought the fight on many fronts and at times we have won a battle or two, but the war is not over.

Almost five years after we moved to Pensacola, Jane and I were thrilled and blessed to become grandparents. Our daughter, Ann, gave birth to Katherine—the first of her three children—on January 7, 1989. Katherine was followed by Walker on July 7, 1993, and Rebecca Ann on October 20, 1999. They would live in a home only a few blocks from us, and we would be very close to them in their developing years.

Another of the wonderful gifts we have received through the years is being blessed to know some of the finest Christian people in the world. We first moved to Pensacola First Church because of Dot Stewart, who was the chairperson of the Pastor-Parish Relations Committee. She introduced herself to me at Annual Conference in June 1984. At the time, she told me that the Church's pastor, Bob Dickerson, had been at the church for ten years and the church was looking for their next pastor. Rebecca was in the tenth grade, and I told Dot that I was honored and would think about it, but the timing was not right for me or my family. She was polite but very firm and told me that we would talk some more. Little did I know that in August of that same year, she would return with the bishop in tow, and I was invited strongly to consider this appointment. It was obvious to me that Stewart and her committee would not take no for an answer, so Jane and I talked through the process and made the decision to move to Pensacola in a mid-year appointment. I was privileged in the latter part of Dot's life and at her funeral to voice my gratitude for her persistence in pursuit of her new pastor. Her daughter and son in law, Lynn and Larry Morris, would become some of our best friends over the years.

There were so many wonderful individuals who came into our lives through the First Church family who are now gone. They include Mary McMillan, Ron and Dot Jane Yeakel, Doug and Sara McCrary, George and Betty Olliff, Bob and Clara Mae Turner, Jack and Carolyn Fleming, George and Blanch Baskin and so many others. The gift of relationships is experienced in the entire network of people who enrich your lives along life's journey, and these are only a sampling of the individuals at First Church who come to mind because I have missed them so much since their passing.

Mary McMillan was a teacher by training, but her real claim to fame was that she served as a missionary to the people of Japan for thirty-four years. She was the last Protestant missionary to leave Japan before the atomic bomb was dropped in Nagasaki and Hiroshima in 1945. She was retired when we arrived in Pensacola, but she was very active in the ministry of First Church and several community causes. Only six months before Mary died, a young Japanese girl came with a tiny baby to a Sunday morning worship service. She was so well-mannered and lovely. After the worship service, I introduced myself to her and in broken English she introduced herself as Mitsuko Igushi. In time I asked Mary, who spoke fluent Japanese, if she would meet her and see if we could help involve her in the Church's ministry. They became dear friends, and Mary helped her develop her English skills. At Mary's funeral, Mitsuko shared with the congregation a couplet that Mary had used to teach her English: "Though love is weak and hate is strong, yet hate is short and love is long." Soon after Mary's death, Mitsu came to see me to say, "I must go back to Japan." I have missed her and often thought of her. I never fully understood why she was in Pensacola or why she returned to Japan. Sometimes I have wondered if she might have been an angel that God sent to be with us when Mary died and help us realize that Teacher Mary belonged both to us and the Japanese people but ultimately to God.

Ron and Dot Jane Yeakel gave Jane and me the use of their wonderful condominium, and at least twice a year, we would pack up and move our girls to Perdido Key. While I would commute to work—about a thirty-minute drive—Jane and the kids would play on the beach that we all came to love. Ron had been a prisoner of war in Germany in World War II and had learned to cherish life. He taught us to enjoy good food and drink and to laugh at life. One of his many stories was about Christmas in the German war camp. All the American prisoners gave Ron their small rations of sugar so he could bake them a cake. He carefully took the finished product out of the oven, and as he was walking to the table, he slipped and dropped the cake on the dirt floor. With tears in his eyes, he would recall sitting down and eating the cake—dirt and all—until the other prisoners came and joined him with delight and much laughter.

Doug and Sara McCrary came to Pensacola from Alabama when he was named president of Gulf Power during a challenging time for that company, but it was not his success as a business leader that touched me. He had grown up in Chilton County, Alabama, and had known hard times just like my father had growing up in the same area during the Great Depression. The loss of my father in the late 1980s and Doug's heritage and presence meant that he filled a great void that I was experiencing in those years. Doug was much like my father, a man who could fix anything that was broken or worn out. He kept most of my old lawn mowers and watches and everything else in good repair. When something broke, I would run by his house, and he would fix it and return it to me cleaned up and sounding like a new machine. I liked telling people that my personal repairman was also the president of Gulf Power. It was Doug who pushed first Jane and then me to write our personal histories for the sake of our children. Keep that in mind, and if you are weary from reading my stories, don't blame me, blame Doug McCrary.

One of the most disciplined individuals I have known was Bob Turner. My brother had encouraged me to start jogging for good health back in early 1970, but it was Bob who became a running partner when we moved to Pensacola. We often ran together in the early morning, and it was Bob who helped me through one of the most difficult challenges in my life. On the Saturday before Labor Day 1993, I was celebrating my fiftieth birthday year by training for the grueling task of running the New York City Marathon when a sleepy driver lost control of her car on Scenic Highway and slammed into me as I ran on the bike trail beside the road. The accident left me with a severed right leg and a number of other broken and rearranged bones. My family and many others— and especially Bob—encouraged me and helped me walk again and even run after two years of rehabilitation. I have always felt that the human body is the temple of God and that we have to nourish it with positive thoughts and nutritious food and keep it strong and healthy with a disciplined diet and exercise. It was this commitment and relationships with people like Bob that restored my life after this debilitating accident. For the most part, I chose to exercise by running because I could do it alone and on my schedule and found that it gave my mind time to relax and air out. Through the years, I was never competitive in my running but used the discipline to stay healthy. This crazy accident in 1993 took away a year and a half of my life for surgery and rehabilitation, but I learned that sometimes it takes being helpless and flat on your back to realize that God is good all the time through all circumstances and that our lives are not something we earn or deserve but a holy gift. As my muscles and knees have weakened over the years, and I have slowed down a bit, I have moved to bicycling to keep healthy. But it was the wonderful people like my brother and Bob who modeled for me that health comes through a disciplined life.

George and Betty Olliff always reminded me, by their living example, of the power of the discipline of prayer. For the two decades of knowing and enjoying them at First Church, I don't think I ever made a significant administrative decision, like changing staff members, for example, without first asking Betty her opinion and if she would pray for everyone that might be influenced by the decision. As I have reviewed my journals and the lives of spiritual giants like so many individuals like the Olliffs, I have realized again the importance of the Methodist Way of the disciplined life. The practice of spiritual disciplines such as prayer, worship and communion, study of both the Bible and other spiritual writings, charitable giving, and acts of kindness, have all made a world of difference in my daily life. Over the past thirty years, I have added the spiritual discipline of writing in a journal, which has become one of the most healthy disciplines and has enabled me to worry less and get concerns out of my mind, give them to God, and get on with life.

Carolyn and Jack Fleming offered to Jane and me a friendship that helped shape and enrich our lives at First Church. While Jack was a respected cardiologist, Carolyn was one of the most creative and sociable individuals I have ever known. A meal with the two of them was always an experience of joy in sharing wonderful stories and memories of places visited and people met. They traveled so much, and you would go to their home to learn of their most recent ventures and before you realized it, they would have you talking about yourself rather than what they had been doing. They did write of their travels in a book entitled, *Thinking Places: Where Great Ideas Were Born*. They encouraged us to travel and enjoy the mystery of meeting new people and experiencing new places. Once they gave us a book *1,000 Places to See Before You Die*, and the truth was I believe they had visited most of those places and sometimes more than once. They also taught us that grace and style is demonstrated by showing interest in others.

Two other individuals in the First Church family who brought abundant blessings to my life and ministry were George Baskin and Pat Brinson. George and Blanch Baskin had moved to Pensacola after George's long and distinguished career in the field of publishing with Word Publishing out of Texas and then Abingdon Press. In the mid-1980s, George had started a new imprint called Russian Resources Press. Over the next five years, they found in Moscow interpreters, type setters, printers, marketers, and warehouses to accomplish all these publishing functions for English Christian classics in the Russian language. They translated, published, and marketed some thirty of these Christian classics, including Bible studies, children's books, and devotional titles. Soon after they arrived in Pensacola, George approached me with an intriguing offer to help me publish some of my sermons through a new publishing house venture of his, the Ardara House, which he had created to channel his creative skills in his retirement years. Through the years, George would also help several of my friends and fellow pastors of large United Methodist Churches in the Alabama-West Florida Conference—Herb Sadler,

Karl Stegall, J.B. Nichols, and Powers McLeod—with similar projects through the Ardara House.

Pat and Jim Brinson were lifetime members of First Church, and Pat used her editorial and grammatical skills to help with every book that George published for me. George's and Pat's efforts would expand my ministry far beyond anything I could have ever imagined. *The Robins are Back*, published in 1992, featured a collection of sermons designed for encouragement. *Life is Gift*, published in 1994, was an expression of gratitude for life after my debilitating accident. It was also translated and published in the Russian language. *On Becoming the Person You Want to Be* was published in 1997 to encourage people to pursue their dreams, and in 2000, *Readings and Reflections about Death and Grief* was published as I dealt with the deaths of family members and friends. The truth is that without George and Pat and their hard work, these books would never have seen the light of day and over the years because of their labor, I have discovered that the written word is a powerful tool of communication.

As we approached the beginnings of the twenty-first century, there was a great deal of fear that our computers might lock up and wreak havoc for the new age. Perhaps the fear drove humankind to ramp up our preparation, but as usual with so much of our fear, it was unfounded. Mark Twain was right when he said, "I've had a lot of worries in my life, most of which never happened." On September 11, 2001, we saw Muslim extremists destroy the World Trade Center and make a direct hit on the Pentagon in Washington, D.C. It was a bloody beginning to an age of uncertainty and war. It was the realization for me that my work was yet undone, but I began to consider the possibility of other younger ministers like Wesley Wachob and my young associate, Geoffrey Lentz, beginning to step up in leadership in my place. After a three-month sabbatical leave in 2003, during which Jane and I traveled to Europe with study time at Christ Church College in Oxford, studying at Claremont Seminary in California as a guest of my friend, Dr. Phil Amerson, who was president of the seminary and for whom I had preached when he served the University Church in Bloomington, Indiana.

After the time away for reflection and rest, we returned to Pensacola where I would serve only three more years at First Church. In early 2006, I announced my planned retirement from a congregation where I had spent more than half of my total years in the ordained ministry. I had come to First Church when I was forty-one years old, and in twenty-three years, I had led 783 worship services, 750 funerals, 463 baptisms, 465 confirmations, and 378 marriages. At sixty two, I still had a wonderful and fruitful ministry, but I was growing weary of the constant demand. The years of conducting funerals for church members who had become a part of my emotional family was increasingly difficult, and the price of pastoral ministry for more than three thousand people was an increasingly heavy burden. Additionally, I had never worked outside of the church, and there was a desire before I fully retired to see if I could make it in a business in the secular world.

In 2006, I retired from the Church's ministry through the Alabama-West Florida Conference of the United Methodist Church to move into a new role as president of the Sacred Heart Health Care System Foundation, which was a large nonprofit Catholic hospital system covering Northwest Florida.

By the time I retired from active church ministry, Jane and I had worked with the Sacred Heart Health System for many years. She already had a long and fruitful career with the Developmental Evaluation Program affiliated with the intensive care unit at Sacred Heart Children's Hospital. The hospital served mothers with high-risk pregnancies and served fragile infants in need of intensive care. In an institution committed to the principle of the Sanctity of Life, the services developed into the highest state of the art of medical programs and support programs for families with at-risk medical circumstances. The Daughters of Charity were leaders in Christlike care as were the physicians and nurses who served God through their work.

Dr. Jimmy Jones was a pediatric surgeon who, with lovely long fingers performed surgery on tiny hearts of two pound infants. Drs. Nagel, Westmark, Bell, and other infant care physicians promoted and cared for the smallest, vulnerable infants in their fragile beginnings. Nurses like Clara Harris, Head RN for the intensive care nursery made sure that infants and their families received the best of God's love and support in difficult circumstances. During this time, Jane researched and grew in understanding of young moms and their abusive and difficult lives and assisted with the developmental needs of their families. Through this, I developed in my care concerns for children, elderly, and the most vulnerable of God's children.

For nine years, I had served on Sacred Heart's board of directors and found there an institution and a means of reaching a larger audience of individuals who were poor and desperate for quality health care. It was a great privilege to raise money to provide medical help for the needy of Northwest Florida, and for seven years I found the work very rewarding. The millions of dollars raised helped build a new hospital in Port St. Joe and new facilities and services in Destin and Pensacola. I would work as a part of the Sacred Heart leadership team until February 2013 when I at last did retire at seventy.

My relationship with Sacred Heart helped accomplish the union of a major health care ministry and an elderly care institution seeking to expand into Northwest Florida. I had tried to add the dimension of an assisted living facility serving the retirement community to the various ministries of First Church for a decade but could never raise the capital to accomplish this much needed service in downtown Pensacola. One day I woke up to the fact that I was in a unique position of sitting on the boards of both Sacred Heart and the Methodist Homes for the Aging of the Alabama-West Florida Conference, and all I had to do was bring the leadership of these institutions together and make this new ministry happen. So many things came together when at last the two CEOs—Wray Tomlin of Methodist

Homes and Patrick Madden of Sacred Heart Health System—met with me to explore the possibility of entering into a partnership for a new ministry for the elderly. Neither did it hinder the process that, at the time, I was the chairman of the board's audit committee at Sacred Heart and knew that this was an easy financial possibility. The long story made short is that we were able to negotiate a complicated but workable contract with these two institutions and create two new assisted living facilities, The Haven of Our Lady of Peace and Wesley Haven Villa. The Haven was a skilled nursing home needing a new building on land already owned by Sacred Heart with Sacred Heart managing the facility and owning 51 percent and Methodist Homes for the Aging owning 49 percent. Wesley Haven Villa, was a new assisted living facility to be located on land owned by First Church. Methodist Homes would manage and own 75 percent while Sacred Heart would own 25 percent. The contribution of the land by the church to locate it in the center of Pensacola surrounded by six large church congregations filled with elderly potential residents sealed the deal, and the rest is history to the benefit of all parties concerned and especially the people of Pensacola.

My second career as a fundraising executive with the Roman Catholic Health Care Ministry made it possible for us to enter the retirement years financially secure and confident that we could live without fear of financial need after our income producing years.

I recently tried my hand at writing an "Investment strategy on a Note Card," which looked like this:

Goal: To build a low-maintenance, low-cost, medium-growth portfolio to fund our retirement years and to fund charitable causes that reflect our values and leave a sustainable amount of money for our children and their families.

To do this, we would keep:

- 55 percent of our investments actively invested in stocks and managed mutual funds for growth

- 30 percent in basic bonds or money markets to sustain our needed cash flow
- 15 percent in secure inflation-protected annuities and savings accounts

Within these parameters, we have committed to:

- Living on the required minimum distributions of our retirement funds and Social Security monies monthly
- Staying out of debt by paying off all credit card debts at the end of every month
- Rebalancing and harvesting the growth of all our investments at the beginning of each year.

Over the six decades of our life journey, Jane and I have practiced a shared philosophy of money management to "save 10 percent, give 10 percent, and spend the rest with joy and thanksgiving." This has created many joys of giving to Christian and humanitarian causes and to having a sustainable financial life to do pretty much whatever we have desired to do over the years. We are conservative with our money and not careless, and I am trying hard to experience the joy of spending and giving and living with abandonment without regard to the cost, which is not easy for me.

My time in retirement has allowed me to reflect over my four decades of service as a part of the United Methodist denomination, I realized with an overwhelming sense of gratitude, the benefits of our connectional system. The ordained ministers I had been privileged to have worked with as associates and the lay leadership in our churches and all the unique individuals throughout the world who have enriched my life came to me through the denominational connection. Throughout the years I have enjoyed opportunities to preach in some of the great churches of our denomination. There was First Church in Phoenix and in San Diego; Hennepin Avenue Church in Minneapolis; Boston University's Marsh Chapel and Chautauqua, New York, as well as churches throughout the Southeastern Jurisdiction. Because of the privilege of experiencing the strength of a denomination that combined evangelism with social concern,

I have no place in my mind for any spirit of disunity or disaffiliation. Such divisive attitudes are contradictory to my understanding of God's will and design for the human family.

I have chosen over these last few years to serve as a volunteer President of the Board of Directors of Bright Bridge Ministries and as President of the Rotary Club of Pensacola. These roles have provided me a wonderful means of reaching across barriers to encourage those in great need to reclaim life's possibilities and to encourage those with abundant resources to use their gifts for the benefit of all.

Conclusion | Eighty and Beyond

Today Jane and I are officially in retirement and traveling to new places unrushed and without agenda. I write with no purpose and allow my mind to follow its own wandering course. For the first time in my life, I am free from goals to reach and tasks to complete. I continue to accept a few new challenges and a few select invitations to speak. I have returned to reading just for the joy of reading rather than looking for sermon illustrations. A number of interesting possibilities continue to present themselves for employment and others for volunteer service, but I am enjoying for the first time since my early teen years—when I threw newspapers—not being responsible for some task or fundraising for some cause. I must confess that I have accepted during this time a few marriages and funerals and speaking engagements because I still find it so difficult to refuse friends or the church or a great cause that will make a difference in our community. I also confess that I worry about our grandchildren and now our great grandchildren, Harper, Asa, and A.J., and continue to seek ways to strengthen their ability to choose worthy goals, avoid drugs, and pursue and achieve their dreams by following the way of Christ.

As I moved emotionally toward the decision of my second retirement in the early spring of 2012, Pope Benedict XVI announced his retirement from the papacy of the Roman Catholic Church by saying "he was retiring to a life of prayer and reflection." When I read his public announcement, his statement affirmed something I have longed for deep inside and seemed to capture my desires for my retirement years. Retiring to a life of prayer and reflection was what I was now ready to pursue with confidence. At the same time, my readings of the musings of the Franciscan Father Richard Roth have most aptly described my inner spiritual longing to live out my days as a "contemplative activist." I have for years felt, as Father Rohr voices in his book "Falling Upward": "We are led by Mystery, which religious people rightly call grace…Those who walk the full journey…are the ones who have heard some deep invitation to "something more," and set out to find it by both grace and daring."

When I began writing these stories and recorded the years and events of our ministry, I thought I would publish these writings as a fifth and final book, but the more I thought about it, I became uneasy that it could be interpreted as a document that was all about me, myself, and I. These stories are about a lot of people who are doing things far more important than anything I have ever done or hope to do. I started out with the love of supportive parents and family, and through the years, I have been the recipient of unlimited opportunities in the communities where I have been privileged to live. My greatest joy has been marrying Jane Strange and raising our children. I have only written these pages so that they might one day have these stories and know that Jane and I have lived to serve and loved and enjoyed all that has been given to us.

God be in my head and in my understanding,
God be in mine eyes and in my looking,
God be in my mouth and in my speaking,
God be in my heart and in my thinking,
God be in my end and at my departing.

—Old English Prayer in Sarum Primer

Epilogue

Some days it is difficult to believe how fast time flies by. Jane and I now look back over almost a quarter of a century since the 20th century became the 21st century. We have the great joy of celebrating more than six decades of our marriage and wonderful family with appreciation for the ministry and life God has given us.

It seems the only constant in life is change. I hold in my hand a small computer called a phone that connects me quickly with the whole world of friends and information. Institutions of family, church, and country are changing. Artificial intelligence is beginning to impact everything, including this document.

We too must change. As an octogenarian I find new direction as a Rotarian. I say with others "Is it the truth? Is it fair to all concerned? Will it build goodwill and better friendships? Will it be beneficial to all concerned?" I seek new ways to spread the love of Christ of many names in our constantly expanding universe.

I conclude this small story with a thankful heart. There is so much for which to give thanks as I express our appreciation to those who have assisted in the publication of these memories of ministry. Special thanks to Jeb Hunt and Henry Neufeld for their publishing skills and Kari Barlow, Ruth Ann Replogle, and Barbie Spears who assisted in editing these pages. How grateful I am for so many other individuals over the years, unnamed, who in their relationship with God shared their blessings, love, and guidance.

It is my prayer that in sharing these stories it will help you find the special calling that God has for you in a time of change.

www.ingramcontent.com/pod-product-compliance
Lightning Source LLC
Chambersburg PA
CBHW030944090426
42737CB00007B/530